west highland white terrier

understanding and caring for your breed

Written by
Tina Squires

west highland white terrier

understanding and caring for your breed

Written by
Tina Squires

Pet Book Publishing Company

Bishton Farm, Bishton Lane, Chepstow, NP16 7LG, United Kingdom.

881 Harmony Road, Unit A, Eatonton, GA31024 United States of America

Printed and bound in China through Printworks International

The 'he' pronoun is used throughout this book instead of the rather impersonal
'it', however no gender bias is intended.

ISBN: 978-1-906305-69-7
ISBN: 1-906305-69-2

Acknowledgements

The publishers would like to thank the following for help with photography:
Tina Squires (Bellevue), Holly Barrington (McHolglyn), and Karen Kibble
(Albacharm).

Page 124 © Sabine Stuewer, Tierfoto (http://www.stuewer-tierfoto.de/)

Contents

Introducing the West Highland White Terrier   8

Tracing back in time   16

Developing the breed   20

What should a Westie look like?   26

What do you want from your Westie   38

What does your Westie want from you?   42

Extra considerations   48

　　Male or female?   50

　　More than one?   51

　　An older dog   52

Sourcing a puppy   54

Puppy watching   62

A Westie-friendly home   68

Settling in   82

House training   88

Choosing a diet   92

Caring for your Westie   102

Social skills   118

Training guidelines   124

First lessons   128

Come when called   132

Stationary exercises   136

Control exercises 140

The ideal owner 146

Opportunities for Westies 148

Health care 156

Common ailments 168

Inherited disorders 180

Introducing the West Highland White Terrier

The West Highland White Terrier, most commonly known as the Westie, is a highly popular representative of the terrier group, renowned for his spirited character.

This little dog with a big attitude is alert, courageous and self reliant, while also being a friendly and charming companion. The Westie's happy, inquisitive, adaptable nature makes him an outstanding companion for people of all ages.

Physical characteristics

The West Highland White Terrier was originally bred as a chase and hunt terrier, going on the trail of fox, badger and otter. To this day, the Westie retains a very workmanlike appearance, with a small compact body,

powerful hindquarters, and short, muscular legs. The distinctive head is broad, with small erect ears, and dark eyes with a singularly piercing expression.

The coat, which is always pure white, has a dense undercoat and a non-shedding topcoat which is harsh in texture. A pet Westie's coat will need to be trimmed on a regular basis, which will require the services of a professional groomer.

For more information, see page 102.

Temperament

As well as being used as hunting dogs, the original Westies were also used to dispatch vermin, such as rats and mice. Although most Westies now lead easy lives as much-loved family pets, the breed has retained the 'ratter's temperament' – as owners will experience when squirrels are spotted on walks in the woods, or a pigeon or cat dares to invade the back garden!

The Westie is self-assured and fearless, but he is also a loving and affectionate companion. It is the combination of these traits that makes the breed so adaptable. The Breed Standard states that the Westie has "no small amount of self-esteem" and this is the perfect description for a small dog that is full of his own self-importance.

A suitable home

The Westie's small size makes him an easy breed to own as far as accommodation is concerned. He will be equally happy in an apartment or in a country mansion, as long as he has a garden to explore, and the opportunity to exercise in different, stimulating environments.

The Westie can be very playful and will enjoy the company of children. However, it is essential that children know how to behave with dogs. Sweet though he is, particularly when he is a puppy, the Westie is not a toy and needs to be treated like a proper dog.

Below: The Westie is a true terrier at heart.

The Westie must learn to respect the children in his family and, just as importantly, children must learn to respect him. If interactions are supervised from an early age, and mutual respect is established, the Westie will make an admirable family companion.

Essentially a working terrier, the Westie will not thrive as a pampered pet. He enjoys his creature comforts, but he also needs regular exercise come rain or shine. For older people, with an active lifestyle, the Westie is a perfect choice.

Gardeners beware!

The word 'terrier' or 'earth dog' comes from the Latin word 'terra' meaning 'earth' – and if you own a Westie, you will soon find out why!

A Westie will watch with great interest while you plant next spring's bulbs and, once you have gone indoors, he will spend an enjoyable 10 minutes digging them up again. There is really nothing to be done about this – it's the nature of terriers!

Living with pets

The Westie is a sociable little dog, and will be more than happy to share his home with other dogs, particularly if they his own kind. Westies understand each other, and get great enjoyment from pursuing

shared interests – as long as they still look to you as head of the family.

A Westie can live in harmony with the family cat, particularly if he learns how to behave around cats when he is young. It is important to bear in mind that he has a strong chasing instinct, and this may well get the better of him, particularly if he sees the neighbor's cat.

Never trust a Westie with small animals, such as hamsters and guinea pigs that are kept as pets. The Westie was used to exterminate vermin, and he will not distinguish between a beloved pet and a pesky rat...

Life expectancy

We are fortunate that the Westie has a good life expectancy and many survive into their teens, even making it to their mid teens.

Good care and management are highly influential factors, so if you work hard at keeping your Westie fit, he will remain active for many years.

Tracing back in time

Small working terriers have been used for hunting and to control vermin for many centuries, and Scotland is famous for the breeds it has produced.

There are five terrier breeds that have their origins in Scotland – the Scottish Terrier, the West Highland White Terrier, the Cairn Terrier, the Dandie Dinmont and the Skye Terrier. With the exception of the Dandie Dinmont these breeds appear to share a common ancestry, and it was some time before they were developed as individual breeds in their own right.

There are records of a small terrier-like, rough coated dog, used to control vermin, that date back as early as the 15th century. It is believed that in the early 17th century, King James I of England requested that County Argyllshire (Scottish argyles originate here) supply "six white earthe dogges" to

be shipped across the channel as gifts for the King of France. This may well be the earliest mention of the West Highland White Terrier.

Poltalloch terriers

The first strains of the West Highland White Terrier are attributed to the Malcolm family from Poltalloch in Argylshire, and date back to the 19th century.

Colonel Edward Malcom, 16th Laird of Poltalloch, wanted a working terrier that could follow fox, badger and otter over the rocky terrain of the highlands. For this, a dog needed to be game, hardy, agile and sure-footed. He also had to be self-reliant and courageous so he could work on his own initiative.

At this time, most of the working terriers in Scotland were red, grey, sandy, wheaten, and sometimes a dirty white color. Most breeders discarded white puppies as they were thought to be weaker than their colored littermates, and some believed they were unlucky.

However, Colonel Malcolm favoured white dogs as he thought they stood out among the heather and rocks of the highlands. In fact, there is a story that one his favorite terriers was shot when it was mistaken for a fox, and so ever afterwards he bred white terriers.

Facing page: The original Poltalloch Eleven kept by Colonel Malcolm at this home in Poltalloch, Argyllshire.

Colonel Malcolm also took great pains to establish the right type of dog for working the difficult terrain of the Western Highlands of Scotland. He would continuously work his dogs in the field and would only select the best dogs for breeding, based on their capabilities and their conformation. In time, he established a complete kennel of white terriers, which were first known as Poltalloch terriers.

Developing the breed

From 1890 onwards a number of white terriers were exhibited at dog shows. They had various names including White Scottish Terriers, White West Highland Terriers, Poltalloch Terriers, and Roseneath Terriers, which were bred on the Duke of Argyll's estate at Roseneath.

Colonel Malcolm was involved in showing his dogs, and with the help of fellow enthusiasts, he established a breed club for the White West Highland Terrier in 1905.

A Breed Standard was drawn up but official recognition from the Kennel Club did not come until a year later when the name was changed, and the West Highland White Terrier Club was formed.

The most successful breeder in these early days was Provost Colin Young of Fort William. In 1907 he had the distinction of breeding and owning the first Champion, Ch. Morven, and he also bred the first female Champion, Ch. Cromar Snowflake, who was owned by the Countess of Aberdeen.

In 1908 Colin Young dominated Crufts when Morven and Snowflake won the dog and bitch Challenge Certificates. These two Westies went on to win the Brace class, their son, Argyle, won Best Puppy, and mother, father and son took the Team prize.

American Westies

The West Highland White Terrier is a thoroughly Scottish breed, but it was not long before news of the white terriers spread overseas. In 1906 there is mention of a show dog in the USA, listed as a Roseneath Terrier, and in 1908, the breed is listed in the American Kennel Club stud book.

The following year, the name was changed to West Highland White Terrier, and the UK Breed Standard was adopted. The West Highland White Terrier Club of America was formed at the same time.

The first American Champion was imported from the UK. Known in the UK as Clonmell Cream of the Skyes, he became Am. Ch. Cream of the Skies.

Facing page: Early winners from the Inverailort kennels, pictured in 1911 with Mrs Cameron-Head.

In the mix

Whilst the breed was being established, it was not unusual for Cairn Terriers and West Highland Whites to be inter-bred. White puppies could be registered as West Highland Whites, the others as Cairns.

In 1917 the American Kennel Club were the first to ban this practice, stipulating that a West Highland White Terrier could not be registered if a Cairn appeared in the first three generations of the pedigree.

In the UK, the move to end inter-breeding with Cairns was highly controversial as many of the top dogs had Cairns in their ancestry. However, the Kennel Club settled the argument by banning breeding between Cairns and Westies from January 1st 1925.

Gong global

Since the early days, the West Highland Terrier has gone from strength to strength, and is a popular show dog worldwide.

The breed has been blessed with some outstanding breeders who have dedicated themselves to producing dogs of the highest quality. It is a mark of their achievements that the breed has been honoured with two Crufts Supreme Champions – Ch. Dianthus Buttons in 1976 and Ch. Olac Moonpilot in 1990.

Today registrations remain strong on both sides of the Atlantic, and the Westie is valued as a great showman, and a wonderful companion.

What should a Westie look like?

The Breed Standard is a picture in words describing the perfect pedigree West Highland White Terrier in terms of character and conformation.

Originally drawn up by pioneers of the breed, the Standard has altered very little in over a century. There are minor differences in wording depending on the governing national Kennel Club, but these do not alter the desired overall appearance of the breed.

The Breed Standard is used by breeders striving to produce dogs that adhere most closely to its stipulations, and by judges who evaluate dogs in the show ring.

Of course, no dog is perfect, but the aim is to reward dogs that conform to the Breed Standard in all its

important aspects. In this way, the West Highland White Terrier remains true to the intentions of those that first established the breed, and as winning dogs are used in breeding programmes, it is hoped that their virtues will be passed on to future generations.

General appearance

The Breed Standard makes it clear that a good example of the breed must still be fit for its original purpose which was the catching and killing of vermin. The West Highland White Terrier, described as having a "varminty appearance", is not just bred to look good; his conformation must be correct so that he would still be capable of working in the rugged conditions of his ancestral home.

The Westie is a strongly-built terrier, with a deep chest, a level back, and powerful hindquarters. He should appear well balanced, combining strength and agility.

Temperament

The description of the Westie's temperament speaks volumes. He should be both gay and courageous, self reliant, but friendly, active and hardy. The phrase "possessing no small amount of self-esteem" sums up the bold character of this little Scottish terrier.

Head

The head is distinctive, and it is this, along with the typical piercing expression, that makes the West Highland White Terrier like no other breed.

The skull is broad and slightly domed; there is a distinct stop, which is the indentation of the forehead just above eye level, and the foreface gradually tapers from eye to muzzle. The jaws are strong and level, and the nose, which should be fairly large, is black.

The head is thickly coated with hair, and is shaped to present a round appearance when viewed from the front.

Eyes

The eyes are almond-shaped and should be very dark brown in color. They are spaced widely apart and are deep-set, offering the best protection from possible injury for a working terrier. The expression is all-important – piercing and intelligent – shining out from a mass of white hair.

Ears

The ears are small and should be set neither too wide, not too close. They should be carried erect, terminating in a sharp point. On the ears, the hair should be smooth and velvety.

Mouth

The teeth are large for the size of dog and should meet in a scissor bite, with the teeth on the upper jaw closely overlapping the teeth on the lower jaw. The lip pigment is black.

Neck

Although the Westie is a small, compact dog, the neck must be sufficiently long to allow for the proper set on of the head, which is carried at a right angle, or less, to the axis of the neck. The head should not be carried in an extended position. The neck is muscular and should thicken towards the base so that it merges into the sloping shoulders.

Forequarters

The shoulders slope backwards and the broad shoulder blades lie close to the chest wall. The front legs are short and muscular and are thickly coated with short hair.

Body

The Westie has a compact body with a level topline. The chest is deep and the loins are broad. The ribs are well arched, allowing the working terrier to squeeze between crevices without getting stuck.

Hindquarters

These are strong and muscular, with hocks bent and set in under the body so they are fairly close together when a dog is standing or moving.

Feet

Interestingly, the Westie's front feet are bigger than his back feet. This stems from his working ancestry when the front feet would have been used for digging. The feet should be thickly padded, and the nails are, preferably, black.

Tail

The characteristic carrot-shaped tail is a feature of the breed. It should be 5-6 in (13-15 cm) in length and covered with harsh hair. The tail should be as straight as possible, and carried jauntily.

Movement

The Westie should move with ease and freedom, with the front legs extending forward from the shoulder, and the drive coming from behind. For a small dog, the Westie should move powerfully, with good reach in front, and strength from the rear.

Coat

A working terrier needed protection from the weather, so the Westie is double coated. The undercoat is like fur and is short and soft; the top coat, which is about 2 in (5 cm) in length, is long and harsh in texture.

Color

Only one color is permitted – pure white.

Size

In the UK, the Breed Standard does not distinguish between the sexes and asks for all dogs to be 11 in (28 cm) at the shoulder. The American Standard says there may be a slight deviation, with females being an inch (2.5 cm) smaller than males, with a size of 10 in (25 cm) being acceptable.

Summing up

The Breed Standard is always open to individual interpretation, both by breeders and by judges. That is why the placing of the same dogs may vary from show to show. However, it is essential that these differences apply to minor points only. In all cases, the West Highland White Terrier must be prized as a small, compact, balanced dog, still fit to do a day's work if required, and showing no trace of exaggeration.

What do you want from your Westie?

The Westie is one of the most adaptable of breeds and will suit most lifestyles. However, you need to make sure that you fully understand the Westie character so you have realistic expectations.

Companion dog

If you are looking for a loyal and loving companion, you will not be disappointed. The Westie will build up a strong bond with his owner, and with all the members of his family. He enjoys being part of all family activities, and his small size means that there is usually space in the car so he can be part of everyday outings.

He is rarely confrontational and, for the most part, he will be happy to accept the rules that are laid down.

As a breed, Westies can be quite vocal, particularly when they are excited. The approach of strangers will be greeted with a series of warning barks, but the Westie is a friendly, outgoing dog, and will make friends in no time.

The Westie is a relatively easy dog to care for, although as a pet owner, you will need to budget for regular trips to the grooming parlour to keep his coat in good order. There is also a price to pay for owning a white dog; your Westie will look stunning when he is clean, but at the end of a muddy walk, you will need to be philosophical!

Show dog

The West Highland White Terrier is a popular show dog, and those that become involved in the show world find it very addictive. However, it is not easy to find a dog that has the quality to make it in the ring.

If you want a show dog, you will need to find a breeder that has had some success in this field. You will need to research the pedigrees of both the mother (dam) and the father (sire) of the litter, going back over at least five generations to see what lies behind their breeding. It is also important to see dogs that are closely related to the puppies, so you can get an idea of type of Westie the breeder produces.

No breeder can sell you a puppy at eight weeks of age with the assurance that he will become a show dog. As the puppy grows, he will change so it is impossible to know exactly how he will turn out. You will be buying a puppy with show potential. This means that the breeder thinks that the puppy may be good enough to show, but cannot guarantee it.

Preparing a dog for show requires a great deal of time and effort, and your presentation and handling in the ring will not be learnt overnight. Go to shows, watch and learn, and get advice from experienced exhibitors. The correct trimming of the puppy can be crucial, so you will need to seek advice. Remember, win or lose, showing must be fun for you and your puppy.

What does your Westie want from you?

Before choosing a dog of any breed, you need to appreciate that certain sacrifices will have to be made. It is a good idea to sit down as a family to discuss all of the pros and cons to make sure you can provide a Westie with a home for life.

The first 12 months of your dog's life will be the hardest for you and your family. Your puppy will be very demanding and will need a lot of your time to learn right from wrong. Socializing is a very important part of a young pup's life; the more time you spend training and socializing your young puppy, the happier he will be later in life.

Westies are a happy and loving breed, with a fair degree of intelligence, so you will need to be firm

but kind. A clever Westie will soon understand what is required of him and how he can best please you. However, if you are too soft with a Westie, he will take advantage of this weakness. If you give him an inch, he will take a mile. So you must remember that "no" means "no".

Giving time

Life gets easier when your puppy matures into a well-behaved adult. But your Westie will still require considerable commitment from you.

As already highlighted, the Westie is very much a 'people dog' and he will be miserable if he is left on his own for lengthy periods. He may not be as needy as a puppy, but this does not mean that you should stint on the time you spend with him.

No dog should be left for any longer than four hours at a stretch. If this is going to be a struggle, you will need to think again.

There are options you can consider, such as doggy dare care or using the services of a dog sitter or a dog walker. However, you need to make absolutely certain that the person you employ is trustworthy and has suitable experience.

When you are at home with your Westie, you should also think about the quality of time you spend with him.

He will be happy to hang out with you, but he will relish the opportunity to have special times –going for walks, playing games, fun training sessions, or even getting involved in one of the canine sports such as heelwork to music or agility.

Some Westies enjoy learning new tricks to show off when visitors come round, others like nothing more than a relaxing grooming session, when they can be sure of getting your undivided attention.

It does not matter what you do with your Westie, as long as you give him the quality time he deserves.

Financial commitment

There are costs involved on owning a dog and while these are not enormous, you still need to make the necessary provisions:

- If you are going to need help with day care, can you afford it?

- If you plan to go on holiday without your Westie, can you cope with the additional cost of boarding kennels?

- Have you budgeted for employing a professional groomer to clip your Westie's coat every six to eight weeks?

- Routine health care, such as worming, vaccinations, and flea control, all cost money, as well as providing a suitable diet.

- Are you going to opt for pet insurance, or will you set aside money for additional veterinary expenses?

Exercise requirements

As one of the smaller breeds, Westies have become increasingly popular as they adapt well to the confines of modern life. However, it should be remembered that although a Westie will be delighted to spend time curled up next to you on the sofa, he is not a lap dog. He needs physical and mental stimulation which can only be provided by regular exercise.

Taking on a dog is a lifetime commitment, so do not go ahead unless you are completely sure you can give your Westie the home he deserves.

Extra considerations

Now you have decided that a Westie is the right breed for you and your family, you need to narrow your choice so you know exactly what you are looking for.

Male or female?

Whether you choose a male or a female is entirely a matter of preference – both sexes will give a lifetime of loyalty and affection.

Mature bitches come into season around twice a year. The season lasts for approximately 21 days during which time you must ensure that she does not meet entire males. These days, responsible dog owners do not allow their pets to roam so the chances of an unwanted pregnancy are remote.

However, when a bitch is in season, it is sensible to exercise her in places where you are less likely to meet other dogs. It may also be a good idea to exercise her on the lead in case she decides to roam.

Mature males will urinate to mark their territory but if you have trained your dog correctly, this should not happen in the house. Westies are friendly dogs and a male is no more likely to be prone to fighting than a female. Your training is key.

If you have no plans to breed from your Westie, neutering may be a sensible option. There are health benefits for both males and females. In most cases, a female is spayed at the midway point between her first and second seasons, and a male is usually castrated at 9-12 months of age. If you wish to consider neutering, ask your vet for further advice.

More than one?

Sometimes people think that it would be a good idea to buy two puppies at the same time "to keep each other company". As a general rule, this is not advisable. Two puppies of the same age mean twice the amount of work, and it is virtually impossible to discipline and train them both to a decent standard.

The dogs will tend to bond with each other more than with you and be 'dog's dogs" rather than 'people dogs'.

There is a great deal of pleasure to be had from owning more than one dog if you have the time to devote to them. I would suggest buying one puppy, rearing and training him and then, when he is about 18 months old, well adjusted and bonded with you and your family, consider getting another puppy.

Bear in mind that if your older dog is a male, it is probably safer to buy a female as your second pet. Two males may sometimes clash whereas a male and a female, or two bitches, usually get on well together.

Remember that you must have your dog castrated and your bitch spayed if you have a mixed sex household in order to prevent accidents happening.

An older dog

You may be thinking about giving a rescued dog a new start in life. This can be very rewarding, but you may also encounter some behavioral problems if a dog has been poorly socialized or even mistreated in his first home.

Of course, it can be that a dog needs a new home through no fault of his own – the owner's death, serious illness, or divorce often result in a dog ending up in a rescue shelter. In this situation, a rescued Westie will simply need time and patience to help him to adjust to a new home. But if he has established behavioral problems, you may be taking on too much, unless you are an experienced dog owner and trainer. The best plan is to find out as much as you can about the dog's background, and spend some time with him at the rescue shelter so you can see if he is likely to fit in with your family and your lifestyle.

Sourcing a puppy

The aim is to buy a healthy specimen of the breed that looks good and has a sound temperament. A well-bred Westie will be a joy to own and live with. Bear in mind when purchasing a dog that you are going to look after that dog all of his natural life, so why not have a dog that you will be proud of?

Getting started

Both the Kennel Club (KC) in the UK and the American Kennel Club (AKC) in the USA have excellent websites that offer a wealth of information about the different breeds as well as advice on choosing a puppy. You will also find details of breed clubs, and if you contact your local club, the secretary will be able to put you in touch with breeders who have puppies available.

The Kennel Clubs also provide a register of breeders, and if you opt for those that who have joined the scheme for assured breeders (KC) or breeders of merit (USA) you have the peace of mind that they have followed an agreed code of conduct.

If you are looking for a show puppy, the best plan is to go to a show so you can see lots of different Westies in the ring. You can work out what type you prefer, and talk to the exhibitors after they have finished competing. If you plan to purchase from this source, it may involve going on a waiting list until a litter is due, but if you are looking for something special you will need to be prepared to wait.

Buyer beware!

Do not be tempted by advertisements in the local paper or on the Internet offering puppies at low prices. There may be many repercussion in buying a cheaper Westie, such as getting a dog with health problems or with a poor temperament. It is never a good idea to buy a puppy on a sudden impulse; always wait for a puppy from a reputable breeder.

Below: Do your homework and spend time finding a responsible breeder.

Questions, questions, questions

When you find a breeder with puppies available,
you will have lots of questions to ask. These should
include the following:

- Where have the puppies been reared? Hopefully,
  they will be in a home environment which gives
  them the best possible start in life.

- How many are in the litter?

- What is the split of males and females?

- How many have already been
  spoken for?

- What health checks have been
  carried out?

- Can you see the mother with her
  puppies?

- What age are the puppies?

- When will they be ready to go to their
  new homes?

All reputable breeders will want to see their puppies grow up in the best homes possible. They are, therefore, careful who buys their puppies, so be prepared to answer questions when you are inquiring about a litter.

You will be asked some or all of the following questions:

- What is your home set up?

- Is your garden securely fenced?

- Do you have children/grandchildren?

- What are their ages?

- What job do you do?

- How long are you away from home?

- What arrangements will be made for your dog when you are at work?

- What is your previous experience with dogs?

- How much exercise will you be able to give your dog?

- Do you intend to go to training/ringcraft classes?

The breeder is not being intrusive; they need to understand the environment you will be able to provide for your new dog in order to make the right match. Do not object to this, the breeder is doing it for both the dog's benefit and also for yours.

Be very wary of a breeder who does not ask you questions. He or she may be more interested in making money out of the puppies rather than ensuring that they go to good homes. They may also have taken other short cuts which may prove disastrous, and very expensive, in terms of vet bills or plain heartache.

Puppy
watching

The best age to see the puppies is about six weeks, when they have developed some immunity to disease. By this stage, they are active and playful, and their individual personalities have started to emerge.

Puppies have periods of activity followed by sleep so, hopefully, you can arrange a time to visit when they are most likely to be wide awake. Take note of their surroundings. The puppies will probably be in a pen, which should be clean and smell fresh. However, if you spend some time with the litter, you will observe some bowel movements, which should be firm. Any sign of diarrhoea would be cause for concern.

The puppies should be plump and sturdy. Coats should be clean and healthy looking, eyes clear and free from discharge and ears should be clean and free from wax or mites, which would show as little black specks.

Before vaccinations, some breeders do not like their puppies to be handled by strangers in case of serious infections. If this is the case, ask the breeder to hold a puppy while you take a close look.

Watch the puppies carefully as they play. You will be looking for lively, confident pups that are prepared to come towards you to investigate. A squeaky toy is useful for provoking a reaction. Be wary of the timid puppy that backs off to the far side of the pen; this type of shyness could become a problem later in life.

It is very important to see the mother of the puppies. She may not be looking her best after rearing a litter, but she should appear healthy and have a friendly temperament. It is unlikely that the father of the puppies will be on the premises, as he will probably belong to another reputable breeder. However, you should be shown photographs or be able to find pictures on the breed club website if he has been a winner in the show ring.

Taking a closer look

The breeder should have been handling the puppies on a daily basis since they were born. They should not be frightened when picked up, although they may wriggle as they will want to get back to their games.

Once a puppy is up on his feet, a breeder will stand him on a table (use a door mat or car mat to prevent slipping) and encourage him to keep still for a few seconds. This is known as 'stacking', and it is the way an expert can assess if a pup has the correct conformation. This is essential if a puppy is being sold with the hope of being shown, but it is also helpful for the pet owner to be able to examine each puppy carefully. A puppy who is used to being handled in this way will be easier to groom, and will also tolerate veterinary examinations.

Tell the breeder about your home lifestyle. If you are having difficulty deciding which puppy to have, the breeder may suggest the temperament most suited to your family situation.

If you have any doubts about the health and temperament of the puppies, their environment or the attitude of the breeder, walk away. A Westie puppy is ready to go to his new home at the age of eight or nine weeks. If a breeder tries to sell you a much younger puppy, refuse the offer as they are not putting the welfare of the puppy first.

Show puppy

If you have been to dog shows and are thinking of entering the show world, additional considerations come into play when choosing a puppy. Often the breeder will be keeping what they consider to be 'pick of the litter'. This will leave you with second choice, but there will often be two or even three puppies in a litter that have potential.

To increase the chances of buying a show dog, you may be able to find a breeder with an older puppy for sale. At five or six months old, the adult teeth will be through and the all-important scissor bite should be evident. It is certainly easier to assess an older puppy as he has the chance to grow and develop. If you are looking for a male, two testicles should be fully descended into the scrotum.

You will also be able to assess the temperament of an older puppy. This is crucial, as the best looking dog in the world will not succeed in the show ring if he does not enjoy being there. You want a puppy that moves with confidence on the lead and is not intimidated by other dogs. Remember that an older puppy that is sold for showing will probably command a higher price.

A Westie-friendly home

You need to plan ahead before you collect your pup, so you have all the equipment, food and toys ready for your new arrival. You will also need to make sure your home and garden are safe and secure. These preparations apply to a new puppy but, in reality they are the means of creating an environment that is safe and secure for your Westie throughout his life.

In the home

You need to look at your home from a puppy's perspective so you can eliminate potential hazards. A pup unsupervised for even a moment can pull or knock things off low tables, get into cupboards or out through doors. Fit secure catches on cupboards to keep cleaning fluids and other toxic substances out of reach, and use baby-gates on external doors and on the stairs to give an extra safety net.

Make sure that all electric wires are secured out of reach, as these are potentially lethal. Bitter Apple spray can be applied to woodwork and other chair legs which will help prevent chewing. If you have anything you value that is easily breakable, move it well out of the way or into a puppy-free zone.

The garden

Make a thorough check of your garden to ensure that it is escape proof. Fences need to be secure with no gaps; you will be surprised at the size of hole that a Westie puppy can fit through.

Side gates should be fitted with a bolt or lock, as it is not unheard of for a puppy to be stolen from his owner's garden.

If you have an ornamental pond or a swimming pool, you will need to take extra precautions. Tragically, there has been more than one case where a puppy has drowned while the owner was in the house and unaware of what was happening. The only safe option is to fence off the pond or swimming pool. Even the most shallow of ponds will need attention; a puppy can drown in a remarkably small amount of water.

Below: A Westie puppy will investigate everything he comes across.

There are a number of plants that are poisonous to dogs, so do some research before you bring your puppy home. You can find a full list on the internet. Weedkillers, slug pellets and pesticides are all highly toxic, so you will have to find other ways to control these garden pests.

If you are proud of your garden, you might consider fencing off the area containing your choice plants and flowers so your Westie can have the run of a part of the garden where the occasional excavation will not cause major damage. If you have a reasonably large patio area, this can be ideal as it is easier to clear up after your dog and keep clean.

Equipment you will need

There are a few essential items you will need to buy before your puppy arrives in his new home.

Indoor crate

First-time owners may worry that an indoor crate is like a cage and is a cruel way to keep a Westie. This is not the case; an indoor crate is an invaluable piece of equipment. Once a puppy has been introduced to a crate, he will come to love it as it will be his own space where he will feel safe and can relax.

You may wish to use the crate instead of a bed – your Westie will be very cosy curled up in a crate with a fleece pad inside. A crate can also be used in the car as a safe way to accommodate your Westie when you are travelling. Many owners find that a crate is a blessing on holiday. It can be used in a hotel room or in a holiday cottage to ensure your dog does do get up to any mischief.

Puppy playpen

You have worked hard at making your home safe – but is it impossible to clear all potential hazards from an inquisitive puppy. It gets even more difficult when your puppy is teething, as he will chew and there is nothing you can do to stop this.

The best solution is to buy playpen. While this an additional expense, it is money well spent. The puppy can be safe and secure while you go about your daily chores, or pop to the shops. When you have time to devote to your puppy, he can come out of the pen.

Generally, if a puppy sleeps in the pen, he will learn to be clean more quickly. Dogs do not like to soil the area where they sleep, so a confined space will encourage house training. It is far easier to lay newspaper or training mats in a pen rather than all over the kitchen floor.

In terms of size, the pen needs to be a minimum of 3 ft by 4 ft and 2 ft in height. (90 cm x 120 cm x 60 cm) This will provide enough room for a bed and toys.

Bed and bedding

You will need a bed for your puppy that is relatively chew resistant. The oval, plastic beds available in most pet shops are ideal. A bed that has a soft, cushioned frame will be no good as puppy can easily chew it, and it will be hard to wash.

A cozy fleece pad or a piece of Vetbed will be sufficient for puppy to sleep on. Remember, the puppy will probably soil his bedding, so it will be best to purchase easily washable items, or items with a removable washable cover.

Make sure you buy some extra pieces of bedding as you will be changing and washing it quite a lot in the first few weeks.

Bowls

Bowls for food and water will be needed. Where water is concerned, many puppies regard the bowl as a toy and will often have fun flooding your kitchen floor. A heavy ceramic bowl can go some way to preventing this.

There are many food bowls available on the market. I would suggest buying a stainless steel bowl with a rubber base. The rubber will stop the bowl from slipping when the dog is trying to eat his food.

Safety gate

Often dogs do not like being shut in a room behind a closed door. A safety gate can be useful for restricting your puppy to the kitchen, for example, without making him feel excluded while you are in another part of the house.

Collar and lead

A collar and lead will be needed when your puppy has completed his vaccinations. A small, soft collar is best to start with so that your puppy can get used to the feel of the collar around his neck before you start to walk him.

Make sure the collar is well made so that the fastenings are safe and will not break. The general rule is that if you can fit just two fingers underneath the collar, the dog will not be able to slip out of it.

As your Westie grows and is walking well on the lead, a collar that is half-metal chain and half-fabric material is recommended, as your Westie will not be able to slip out of it.

I suggest two leads – a short one for walking on pavements and near roads, probably about 3 ft (90 cm) long, and a flexi-lead for walking in open areas.

Do not use a flexi-lead near roads as, tragically, there have been accidents where dogs have run into the traffic, and their owners have not been able to control them.

Toys

You will be tempted to shower your Westie puppy with toys, but you need to bear in mind that safety is of paramount importance. Anything that is soft and fluffy will not last, and soft, plastic toy are dangerous if bits are chewed off and swallowed. You need to select sturdy toys that will withstand chewing.

You do not have to spend lots of money on toys – your Westie will get just as much pleasure from knocking an empty plastic bottle (minus the cap) around the garden as he does from an expensive toy. Empty cardboard boxes can also be wrecked, and then thrown away, with no cost involved. Knotted up socks make excellent mock rats for vigorous shaking games.

Hard, rubber toys, such as kongs, are a good choice. You can fill a kong with tasty treats, which will keep your puppy entertained. This is particularly useful for times when you need to leave him in his crate when you go out. However, do not over do it with treats as they may cause an upset tummy.

Grooming gear

A good quality metal comb and a small puppy slicker brush are all that is needed for grooming when you first get your puppy. You can add to this, maybe seeking the advice of your puppy's breeder, as his coat grows.

ID

Your Westie should wear an ID tag when he is out in public places. This can take the form of an engraved disc (with your contact details), attached to his collar. Alternatively you can get your phone number embroidered on to the collar, which is the safer option as a disc is easily detached when a Westie is busy exploring in undergrowth.

You should also have a permanent form of ID such as a microchip or a tattoo. This could make all the difference in finding your dog if he is lost or stolen.

Your veterinary surgeon will be able to micro-chip your dog; this is a simple procedure which involves a small chip being inserted behind your dog's shoulders. This chip carries a unique number which can be identified by a scanner. It is a quick process and relatively painless.

Ear tattoos are more visible. An ear tattoo is a unique range of numbers and letters, which is usually done in black or green ink. It is a simple process to carry out and your vet can point you in the direction of your local dog ear tattooist.

Finding a vet

Register with a vet before you collect your puppy. Ask neighbors and friends with pets where they go and what they think of the service they receive. If your puppy's breeder lives locally, you can seek advice.

Find a practice that is near enough to get to quickly in an emergency. The biggest practices are not necessarily the best; you may find a smaller practice that you feel a lot happier with. You need to have a good relationship with your vet as your trust and confidence in him may be very important at some point in the future.

Settling in

When you collect your puppy, plan to have three or four days free so that you can devote plenty of time to the new arrival. If possible, collect your puppy early in the day so he has plenty of time to adjust to his new surroundings.

It is a daunting experience for a puppy to be taken away from his littermates and everything that he knows. He will need time and guidance from you, so that the transition is as smooth as possible.

To start with, allow the puppy look around his living area while you keep talking to him, using his name and praising him. He will quickly respond to your voice and start following you around. Let him follow you in the garden for more exploration.

Resist the temptation of inviting relatives and friends round to see the pup. This would probably frighten the pup and make his homecoming traumatic. Let the puppy settle in for a week or so and then gradually invite family and friends round to see him.

Westies and children

Within your own family, try to keep introductions calm and quiet. If you have children, do not allow loud screams of excitement and sudden movements, to give to the dog, as this can frighten the puppy.

The best plan is to have the children sitting on the floor, so there is no danger of dropping a wriggly puppy. Give each child a toy or a treat, and allow the puppy to get to know each one in turn. Make sure that all interactions are supervised as it only takes a second for a game to get out of hand, which could harm a puppy or frighten a child.

Introducing house pets

If your puppy is joining an older dog, take care with initial interactions. Take them both into the garden for their first meeting, as your older dog may feel that he has to guard the house.

If your older dog is boisterous, you may want to put him on a lead so that the puppy does not get knocked over and hurt. But try not to interfere too much as the pair need work out their relationship.

For the first few days your older dog is likely to growl at the young pup. This is simply the adult's way of asserting his authority. If your puppy does not take

Dogs are best if they are left to work out their own relationship.

the growl as a warning and continues to pester the older dog, take the pup away for a short spell.

Never leave the two dogs together if you have to go out, and make sure you give equal attention to both dogs to avoid jealousy. Once acquainted, your older dog will be delighted with his new friend.

If you have a cat, it is your puppy that will need

controlling. No cat will put up with being jumped on by an excited puppy, so you need to intervene by distracting the pup's attention and praising him for ignoring the cat. If the first meetings are carefully supervised, both will settle into a routine based on mutual respect.

The first night

For the first few nights the puppy is in his new home, your sleep may be broken by piteous howls from the kitchen. He is having to get used to a totally different situation as he has been used to sleeping with the warmth and comfort of his littermates. However, he must now learn to adapt to his new home, and this has to be done without too much input from you.

Do not scold the puppy, as he is just feeling lonely. Equally, do not pick him up and comfort him. He is clever enough to work out that making a noise will result in a pleasant five-minute cuddle and he will never learn to be quiet. If you do go to him, just put him back in his bed, tell him to "stay" in a very firm voice (he probably won't but, keep trying) and leave. After a few nights, your puppy will settle without making a fuss.

Establishing a routine

Your puppy will spend a lot of time sleeping as he has all the stimulation of a new environment and new people, and he is also growing at a great rate. When he crashes out after a period of activity, make sure he is not disturbed as he needs to rest.

Routine is very important for a puppy, just as it is for a baby. You will have a happy and contented puppy if he is woken at roughly the same time each day, if he has set mealtimes and if he goes to bed at the same time each night. As he gets older, he will appreciate having his walks at roughly the same times each day.

House training

This is the bit that most first-time puppy owners dread, but it does not have to be an ordeal if you establish a routine and put in some hard work for the first few weeks.

A young puppy needs to be let out to relieve himself at the following times:

- First thing in the morning

- After meals

- After play sessions and periods of activity

- Last thing at night.

Do not expect your puppy to go for longer than two hours before giving him the opportunity to relieve himself; the more times he gets it right, the quicker he will understand what is required.

To aid house training, take your puppy to the same area of the garden, and use a cue, such as "Busy" when he performs. Soon he will associate the word with the action and will know what you want him to do. When he obliges, praise him lavishly, and maybe give him a treat.

Do not rush back into the house as soon as your puppy has relieved himself or he may start to use delaying tactics to prolong his time outside. Instead, have a quick game with him – which is another way of rewarding him for co-operating – and then head back to the house.

When accidents happen

Inevitably, there will be accidents in the house, but if you come back from the supermarket and find your puppy has spent, there is no point in scolding him as he will not know what he has done wrong. Rubbing a puppy's nose in his mess is an old-fashioned, unpleasant practice which does no good whatsoever.

If you catch him in the act, say "No" in a firm voice, and swiftly remove him to the garden. He will probably have done what he needs to on the floor before you can get him outside, but at least you will be getting the idea across.

Given a regular routine and plenty of opportunity to go outside, a Westie puppy will learn be clean quite quickly. However, stock up on newspapers and keep the mop and bucket handy!

Right: If your puppy makes a mistake with his house training, it is often your lack of vigilance that is to blame.

Choosing a diet

In order to thrive, a Westie needs a good-quality, well-balanced diet that is suited to his age and lifestyle. There are hundreds of proprietary dog foods available, so how do you know which one to choose?

Initially, it is a good idea to follow the recommendations of your puppy's breeder, as they will have experience in knowing what suits Westies. If this diet works well for your puppy, there is no reason to change it.

However, you may find the brand that is recommended is not readily available in your area, or you feel your dog will do better on a different diet. If this is the case, you may change the food, after your pup has had a month or two to settle in. The food must be changed gradually, over a period of five to six days, mixing in the new food a little at a time. Hopefully this gradual transition will avoid stomach upsets.

When it comes to choosing a diet, most owners opt for a complete, dry food. This is popular as it requires no preparation and can be stored easily. It is specially manufactured to cater for all your dog's nutritional needs so there is no need to supplement. You can buy a diet for your Westie's lifestage, such as puppy, junior adult or senior, and there are also prescription diets for dogs with specific health problems.

Canned food or 'wet' food, which comes in a packet, is another option to consider. This is usually fed with biscuit, which is good for your Westie's teeth. However, these diets do have a high moisture content, so you need to check the ingredients carefully to ensure your Westie is getting the nutrition he needs.

If you have the time and the inclination, the idea of feeding your dog a natural diet made up of fresh meat, cereal and vegetables may appeal. However, make sure you research thoroughly before going down this road. You must ensure that your diet provides all the protein, vitamins, oils and minerals that are included when you feed a branded food.

Regardless of what diet you are feeding, fresh drinking water must be available at all times.

Adult feeding

At about 10 or 11 months, you can put your Westie on the feeding regime which will suit him throughout his adult life. You may decide to feed a small 'token' breakfast and a main meal at around 5pm. Alternatively, you could divide the food equally between breakfast and teatime. Either way, two meals a day is ideal for a Westie. Treats at lunchtime or just before bed are not necessary; too many treats will lead to obesity.

Puppy feeding

At first, your puppy will be on three or four small meals a day. He may find the move to a new home a bit stressful, but if he goes off his food, do not worry.

It is best not to fuss him and give him different foods, otherwise he will learn that if he does not eat, he will be given something better. The result of this will be that you end up pandering to a fussy eater for the duration of your Westie's life.

Below: Choose a good quality diet that is suited to your Westie's age and lifestyle.

Most puppies eat better if they are cut down to two good meals a day by the age of five to six months. Obviously, as you reduce the number of daily meals, the amount given should be increased. The aim is to have a plump puppy that is building up good bone structure and substance for adult life. While the puppy is growing, diet is vital – what you put in at this age will be the making of the adult.

Dangers of obesity

The ideal weight of your Westie will vary according to sex. A small bitch could be around 17 lb (8 kg) whereas a strong male could be 22 lb (10 kg). Watch out for signs of your dog being overweight.

A roll of fat lying behind the shoulders, or on the back just ahead of the tail, indicates that a little less food and a little more exercise are called for. You should be able to see a 'waist' if your Westie is at the correct weight.

An overweight dog is not an attractive sight and, more importantly, obesity has serious health implications. You are literally killing your dog with kindness if you feed him too much, or give him an inappropriate diet. Therefore, you need to work out the correct balance between the amount of food you are giving compared to the exercise he is getting.

A dog that is obese will not enjoy his life to the full – and his life will be shorter. There are many effects of obesity they can include organ malfunctions, skeletal problems, loss of vitality and skin diseases.

For the sake of your dog's health and well-being, resist the temptation of treating him to a piece of your digestive biscuit or cake – a piece of raw carrot is just as welcome to your dog and will not put on the pounds.

Foods to avoid

Many human food can be poisonous to dogs. They include the following: chocolate, onions, raisins and grapes. Cakes and biscuits should be avoided as they contain high levels of fat and sugar.

If you have a cat, you will find your Westie will show a great liking for its food as it is very appetizing. However, it is too rich and has too much protein in it for a Westie, and will result in an upset stomach.

Bones and chews

Your local butcher may sell raw bones and this can be useful when a puppy is teething. Bones will also help to keep teeth clean and healthy in adult life. However if a puppy or an adult has a bone for too long it can cause a stomach upset, but five minutes twice a day usually does no harm.

Never give your Westie cooked bones as these can splinter and cause your dog a lot of damage. Nylon bones can be bought at pet shops and are an acceptable and less messy alternative to the real thing, although your Westie may not be as enthusiastic.

It is not advisable to give pigs' ears, or hide bones and chews. These type of chews can be dangerous as they reduce in size as the dog chews them. The dog may try to swallow the remains, which can stick in the throat and cause a blockage, leading to choking and even death.

Caring for your Westie

The Westie is not a difficult breed to care for, but he does have special requirements, particularly in relation to coat care, that you need to take on board.

Grooming is vital to your Westie throughout his lifetime. A Westie does not shed his coat, so every 8-12 weeks he will require trimming. In between visits to the groomer, your Westie will need daily coat care to keep him in good condition, and to prevent mats and tangles forming. It is therefore important that your Westie gets used to being groomed and handled from an early age.

Puppy grooming

You will need to teach your puppy to stand still on a table, and not to wriggle or bite while he is being groomed. Perhaps try grooming him when he is tired, such as after a period of play or following a short walk. If you stand your puppy on top of a non-

slip mat – a rubber car mat will serve the purpose – you will find it will be easier for him to stand still. You will need to use firm control when grooming, but the experience must still be fun. If need be, why not ask a friend to hold your puppy while you groom him, just until he gets use to the process?

Remember to praise your puppy if he does stand still and behaves himself. If he is naughty, just try to carry on, ignoring his antics. Do not let him win by stopping, otherwise he will realize that if he plays up, you will stop grooming him. This will result in an unmanageable adult, and every grooming session will be a nightmare.

Clipping

You will need to find a good groomer who knows how to do the proper Westie trim. It may be that your puppy's breeder specializes in clipping Westies, but if this is not the case, or the breeder does not live locally, you can ask your vet for a recommendation.

Your pup will first need to go to the groomer when he is about four months old. This means the puppy gets used to being clipped at an early age and he is easier for the groomer to handle.

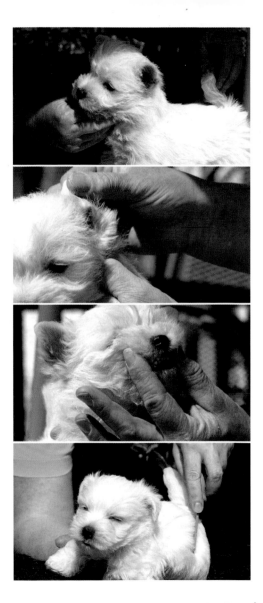

A Westie puppy needs to get used to being handled.

Next, go through the coat with a comb.

Part the lips and examine the teeth.

Accustom your puppy to being groomed.

A clipped Westie looks very smart, but the process of clipping does change the texture of the coat so it is not suitable for show dogs.

Hand-stripping

All show Westies are hand-stripped, which involves plucking out the dead hair with finger and thumb. It is a laborious business, and is better done over a period of time rather than trying to achieve the finished result in one go. You can learn to hand-strip yourself, but you need a lot of time and patience to learn.

A trimming table will be needed, and it is useful to have a trimming arm so you can put a noose around the pup's neck to hold him securely on the table. You may need to get a friend to hold your puppy while you start to strip him.

The adult coat needs to be hand-stripped, plucking out the dead hair with finger and thumb.

Move down the neck to the shoulders.

Work along the back to the hindquarters.

Finish by stripping the tail.

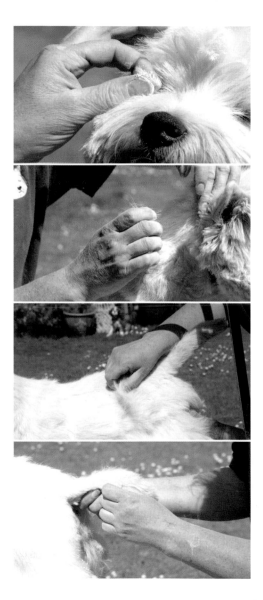

As you start to strip the coat, allow the pup to chew on a dental stick or a chew to keep him sweet and to take his mind away from the stripping. This must be a good experience for your puppy, so be patient.

Only work on the coat for 15 minutes at a time, so pup can get used to the experience. Always end each session on a good note – maybe have a little play with your pup or make a fuss of him, if he is good. Your pup will soon learn what is required of him and he will learn that grooming is a pleasurable experience.

Once your pup has been fully hand-stripped, you must work on his coat weekly to make sure that his hard coat comes through, especially on his back. You may use scissors to tidy up and to shape his furnishings. Clippers are normally used on the dog's front, and scissors around his hindquarters.

By the time your pup is six months, he should have a good coat ready for showing. If you do not work on the coat from a young age, by the time you show your pup he will have a really tatty looking coat that will look a mess in the show ring. When the puppy is old enough to show you want a harsh, tight-looking coat on his back, with short thick furnishings on the legs and head. This will make the puppy look very smart.

Great skill is required to trim the hair on the head to the correct shape.

The hair of the legs is tidied.

Moving to work on the back legs.

Trimming the tail to its correct 'carrot' shape.

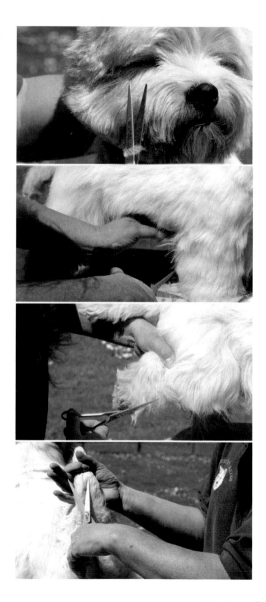

Bathing

Westies do not benefit from frequent baths as this removes the natural oils from their skin and coat. Your groomer will probably bath your dog every time he has a trim, so there is probably no need to bath him yourself. When a puppy is small, an alternative to a bath is to use a few baby wipes to dampen the coat, then shake on some talcum powder and brush. You can also use the 'talc and brush through' method with an adult, which will freshen up the coat in between trips to the groomer.

On the occasions that your Westie needs a bath due to rolling in something undesirable, make sure you use a good quality dog shampoo.

Signs of good health

When you groom your dog you should get into a routine of checking him all over. Look for lumps and bumps, cuts, evidence of parasites such as ticks, and skin irritations. If you spot problems at an early stage, they will be far easier to resolve. Look out for the following signs of good health:

- A cold, damp nose, with no discharge (a small amount of clear fluid is fine), or crustations

- A shiny coat with no bare patches

- Clear, bright eyes with no discharge

- Clean ears that do not look or smell dirty

- Clear skin with no redness or visible irritations

- A firm well-muscled body

- Nails that are well trimmed

- Breath that does not smell unpleasant

Routine checks

There are a number of routine tasks which you need to carry out on a regular basis to keep your Westie in good condition.

Teeth

When a puppy is four weeks old, he will start to develop his first set of teeth, known as milk teeth. The milk teeth will be kept until the puppy starts teething – between the ages of four and seven months. It is a good idea to check your puppy's mouth at this time as sometimes milk teeth may become lodged.

It is important that an adult dog's teeth and gums are kept in good condition, or teeth may have to be removed later in life. You can help maintain your Westie's teeth by brushing them. Many pet stores sell doggy toothpaste and brushes to help you with this.

If your Westie does develop tartar, his teeth will need to be scaled by your vet. Never attempt to do this procedure yourself as you could easily puncture the dog's gum which will lead to infection.

Ears

You will need to check ears on a regular basis as a Westie is always poking his head into places where dirt and mites can be picked up.

Check the ears for any odor or dirt. You can clean them with cotton wool (cotton) and a cleaning product that can be obtained from pet shops or from your veterinary practice. If your dog's ear is infected it will be red, inflamed and may have an unpleasant odor. In this instance, consult your vet so your Westie can be prescribed with the correct treatment.

Nails

You need to check your Westie's nails, and trim them when necessary. This can be done using guillotine type nail clippers, making sure you only remove the tip of the nail. If you cut off too much nail, it causes the quick (the blood vessel in the nail) to bleed.

If you do not feel confident enough to do the job, it is best to ask your vet or a professional groomer to do it for you.

Exercising your westie

Being an adaptable fellow, a Westie will make do
with a walk around the block if the weather is bad,
but once full-grown, this active little terrier will
enjoy a day's walking in the countryside – and will
only need to take a break when you do!

As a general rule, a 30-minute walk twice a day will
suit an adult dog and will also improve your own
health. However young puppies, six months and
below, should only be exercised for 10-15 minutes a
day. As your pup gets older, you can gradually build
up his walk time.

The older westie

The ageing process can start to take hold between
the ages of seven and ten years old. Of course, this
can be accelerated if proper care is not taken of your
Westie, or if he is overweight.

As your Westie ages, you will notice that he will start
to slow down, and he will not need so much exercise.
Do not tire him out with long walks where he is
struggling to keep up. Instead, go for short trips
where your Westie has the opportunity to find new
scents, which he will find stimulating.

Remember to keep a check on your Westie's nails, as, with less exercise, they will not wear down naturally.

Less exercise will also mean that you will need to alter your Westie's diet otherwise weight will pile on, the joints will suffer and many health problems will arise. You may consider changing your Westie's diet to a food that is more suitable for an elderly dog. There are lots of veteran or senior dog foods on the market to choose from.

You may find that your ageing Westie has problems with his eyesight and his hearing. If you notice a greyish tint in your Westie's eyes, he may have cataracts. These days, cataracts can be surgically removed.

At present there is no treatment for hearing loss in the older dog. However, you can help him by giving hand signals as commands.

Stiffness in the joints is likely to occur, so make sure your Westie does not sleep near any cold drafts and that he has have a warm, comfortable bed to sleep in. A supplement of cod-liver oil can aid stiff joints, and in severe cases your vet can prescribe a drug such as glucosamine.

Be sensitive to the needs of your ageing Westie.

Older dogs can be prone to tumors and cysts, most of which will be harmless. However, if a lump is growing rapidly, or there is anything else that concerns you, consult your vet.

In my experience, bringing a younger dog into the home can sometimes give your older Westie a new lease of life. Just remember that as long as you take care of your elderly dog, he will be content and comfortable in his older years.

Letting go

Unless your Westie dies at home from natural causes, you have one last duty to your friend. When the time comes you must, with your vet's agreement, ensure that your Westie is saved from prolonged suffering or pain.

The decision will be hard to make, but in your heart you will know that it is the right thing to do. Your Westie will have given you many years of love and devotion and in return, you must do him this final kindness.

Dog Expert | 117

Social skills

Your puppy's breeder should have started the process of socialization, equipping him to deal with new situations with calmness and confidence. This will be the foundation of how he views the world, and it is your job to continue the work so that he matures into a happy, adaptable adult.

Socializing your puppy from a young age is very important. There have been too many times when a breeder has sold a boisterous, happy-go-lucky puppy, and when the owners have bought him back to show his progress, he has turned into a nervous puppy. This is not due to bad treatment, but to lack of exposure to new experiences. This results in a shy, nervous dog that cannot cope with the stresses of everyday life. In a worst case scenario, you could even end up with an aggressive dog. An adult dog with this frame of mind will, of course, be very unhappy.

Socializing at home

Socializing can start straight away – just give your puppy a day or two to settle in his new home. You can start the process slowly by introducing your puppy to things around the house that he may not have encountered before. Items such as a washing machine or a vacuum cleaner can be scary for a young pup. Make sure the experience of seeing and hearing new things around the house is positive and rewarding.

Take your puppy over to the washing machine (or something he may find frightening) and hold him in front of it. If he wriggles and cries, do not worry; it is not hurting him. Talk to your puppy and reassure him until he realizes the object is not frightening and so he can relax.

Accustom your puppy to being handled regularly by you, and by visitors who may come to your home. Place him on a non-slip mat and let friends and family say hello to him, picking up his paws and checking his teeth and ears. You will need to hold him firmly, but the experience must still be fun and enjoyable.

If your puppy cries and tries to move, hold him on the table until he calms and becomes submissive. Your puppy needs to learn to stand still and co-operate, otherwise you will end up with an aggressive adult that cannot be handled.

It is also a good idea to accustom your puppy to accepting your presence at mealtimes. You can do this by adding food to his bowl when he is eating. This will teach him that you are not a threat and he does not have to 'guard' his food bowl.

Socializing outside

When your puppy is fully vaccinated, you will be able to take him out of his secure home environment to encounter more challenging situations. It is a good idea to take your Westie to a different place a few times a week, so he may become accustomed to a variety of different environments. The more your Westie observes in the first six months of his life, the more confident he will be later in life. Places such as garden centres, pet shops, the surrounding streets and a variety of local parks are good places to visit.

If you find your pup is a little nervous, do not pick him up and take him home – just find a place to sit and let him watch the passing scene. You can reassure him with treats or his favorite toy. If you have an older dog, take him along, too, as he will give the puppy added confidence.

Once your puppy is allowed to venture out, you will want to make sure that he has the opportunity to socialize with other people and dogs. When you are out for a walk, interaction with other dog owners and their pets will add to his confidence – but make sure that the other dog (and his owner) are friendly.

There will probably be a training class in your area and this is an excellent place to socialize your puppy and teach him basic rules. Be careful when you are out walking, or at a training class, that your puppy is not scared by a much larger dog or puppy. Although the other dog may be friendly and mean no harm, being knocked over by a boisterous giant can cause a fright and loss of confidence that takes months to repair.

The more often you take your puppy in the car, the less likely it will be that he suffers from travel sickness. It is advisable not to feed him an hour or two before car travel while he is getting used to the motion of the car.

Right: The aim is for your Westie to take all new situations in his stride.

Training
guidelines

In order to have a well-behaved Westie, you need to be prepared to take on the responsibilities of training and socializing.

You must always remember that you are the leader and that your Westie will look to you to learn right from wrong. Do not let your Westie rule the roost, otherwise you will end up with an unmanageable adult. However, with proper discipline, love and attention, you will have a wonderful little dog that you will treasure forever.

Training needs to be a fun experience for your dog. If your Westie does not enjoy training, he will not co-operate and he will be a lot harder to train. Bear in mind the following points when you are training your Westie:

- Find a reward your Westie values, such as tasty treats or a favorite toy, so he wants to work for you.

- Do not train if you are in a bad mood or you are short of time. The session will not work and you will just end up in a worse mood than when you started.

- Find a training area that is free from distractions. Make sure all other family members and dogs are out of the way.

- Keep sessions short. Long sessions will bore a puppy and will be too much for him to take in. Training for 10 minutes, three times a day, is a good way to start.

- Choose your training times with care. If you use treats to reward your dog, make sure he is a little hungry and that you have not just feed him. A tired dog will not be as easy as a dog that is fresh and alert.

- Pick the right food treat. The treat will need to be small and soft and easy to swallow. All treats will need to be rationed from your dog's daily diet.

- Change the reward and the training area.

- Remember, treats do not need to be used all of the time, you can use a favorite toy or just praise your dog.

- As your Westie matures, start to train him in different places so he will get used to obeying you in every situation.

- Never end a session on a bad note. Try getting your Westie to do something easy so you both feel good because something positive has been achieved.

First lessons

A Westie pup is quick to learn, and he will enjoy the stimulation as well as being rewarded when he gets something right.

Wearing a collar

It is never too early to get your puppy used to wearing his collar. Give him a day or two to settle in his new home, and then try putting it on, making sure it is fitted correctly. You should be able to fit two fingers under the collar without it being too slack.

Your pup will probably start to scratch at his neck quite persistently. Don't worry about this, it is perfectly normal. It is purely because of the strange feeling of having something round his neck for the first time. This should only last a few days.

Lead training

Some Westies take to this straight away, but others will take a little longer to train. It is a good idea to start the process of lead training as early as possible. It must be an enjoyable experience, so

never drag or pull your puppy. Try the following steps:

- Let your puppy run around with the lead attached, play with him and reward him with a tasty treat, such as some chicken.

- Hold the lead and encourage your puppy to follow you while tempting him with the chicken. If he follows you, praise him and make a lot of fuss of him. This will make him associate lead walking as fun and he will enjoy being with you.

- If your puppy fails to follow you, be patient and keep tempting him with the chicken, encouraging him in a high-pitched voice.

- Try carrying him to the end of the garden and then putting him down and head walk off towards the house. You should find that your pup is keen to follow.

Whenever your Westie co-operates and walks on a loose lead at your side, remember to praise him lavishly. He will soon associate walking with you on the lead as a fun, enjoyable experience.

Your puppy will be a willing pupil if you progress in easy stages.

Come when called

This is an important exercise to master for both of you. A Westie with a reliable recall will enjoy the benefits of free-running exercise, and you will have the pleasure of taking your Westie on new excursions, knowing he will always come back to you.

Hopefully, your puppy's breeder will have started recall training simply by calling the litter at mealtimes, or when they were being let out of their pen. You can build on this as soon as your puppy arrives in his new home. He will be feeling a little insecure, so you can capitalise by calling him to you, and giving him lots of praise.

You can also use the "Come" command when your puppy's food is ready or when you have one of his favorite toys. This will teach him to focus on you, and he will get an instant reward when he co-operates.

You can then move into the garden and test his response in an environment where there are more distractions. Make yourself sound fun, calling your Westie in a high-pitched, exciting voice so he wants to come back to you. Make sure he is always rewarded, so he builds up a strong and positive association with the "Come" command.

The outside world

As the distractions increase, it is harder for your Westie to focus on you, so do not try letting him off-lead until you are certain that he will come back. In the meantime you can use a training line, approximately 16 ft (5 metres) in length to improve his response.

- Attach the training line to your puppy's collar, and let him have a run and play.

- Give the "Come" command and give a gentle tug on the lead. When your Westie comes towards you, move away calling him enthusiastically.

- As soon as he gets up to you, give him a treat and lots of praise.

- Keep repeating this method until you are satisfied with your dog's response. If you find he is ignoring you, give a slightly firmer tug on the lead to make him come.

When you have built up a reliable recall, you can let your Westie off the lead for a free run, knowing that he will come back to you on command.

Stationary exercises

These are simple exercises and if you are clear, concise and consistent in your training, a clever Westie will soon understand what is required.

When training your Westie, you must give clear commands, and always use the same verbal cue for an exercise. For example, if you want your Westie to go into the Down position, the cue is "Down", not "Lie Down", or "Get Down". It may mean the same to you, but a Westie will spot the difference and become confused.

Praise lavishly when your puppy has followed a command and never be impatient if he does not appear to be listening to you. Try again, and make yourself sound fun so your Westie thinks it is all a big game. Reward him with a treat, and remember, you can also praise him verbally and by stroking him. At the end of every training session, finish with a play and lots of fuss so your puppy knows you are pleased with him.

Sit

This is a simple exercise, and can be used in lots of different situations.

- Gain your puppy's attention with a tasty treat, and hold it just above his nose.

- As your puppy looks up at the treat, he will naturally go into the sit position. You can now give him the treat.

This lesson must be repeated until your puppy is sitting on command, without needing to be lured into position. Remember you do not always have to reward with a treat. When your Westie understands an exercise, verbal praise will suffice.

Down

Once your puppy has mastered Sit, he is ready to can learn the Down position. This command is very important as an instant response could be a lifesaver.

- Firstly get your puppy into the sit position and gain his attention.

- Hold a treat in one hand, just under his nose. As you say the "Down" command, bring the treat slowly down to the floor.

As your Westie gets more proficient, he will be able to "Stay" in position, despite distractions.

- As your puppy tries to get the treat, he will go into the Down position. This may take a few moments, so be patient.

- As soon as puppy correctly completes the command, make a real big fuss of him and reward him with the treat.

This command will need to be repeated many times before your puppy will do it on his own.

Control exercises

These exercises call for a degree of self-control, which is not easy for a lively puppy. To help him learn, work in short bursts, interspersing the training with lots of play.

Stay

It is easier if you teach this exercise with your puppy on the lead so you can control him.

- Ask your Westie to "Sit", and step away from him. You should have your back towards your Westie and, with your arm stretched behind you, give a hand signal – palm flat, towards your Westie.

- If your puppy moves, correct him by putting him back in his previous position. If your dog has correctly stayed in position, return to him and praise him.

- When your Westie understands what is required, introduce the verbal cue, "Stay".

- Carry on with this method and up the number of steps that you take, but do it gradually. It may take weeks for your dog to master this command.

Be patient when training this exercise. If you find that your Westie is starting to move after you have taken two steps, go back to basics and take just one step. You need to be firm but fair, and always praise well. Remember that if you give your Westie an inch, he will take a mile. But it is equally important to bear in mind that you must never bully your dog. Training must be fun for both of you.

Wait

This is similar to the Stay exercise, as you want your Westie to remain in position, but as you are using a different verbal cue, and a different hand signal, he will understand that this exercise is different. It does not mean a prolonged Stay; it means: "Wait in position until I give the next command".

This command has many uses, such as when you want your dog to "Wait" rather than barging through a door in front of you. But its most important use is commanding your dog to "Wait" in the car so you can clip his lead on before allowing him to get out. A good response to the "Wait" in this situation is a certain lifesaver.

You can train this exercise with your dog on lead to start with:

- Ask your dog to "Sit" and take one step away, this time facing your Westie. With a bent arm, give a hand signal, palm held flat, towards your Westie.

- Step back and reward.

- Keep practicing and when your Westie understands what is required, introduce the verbal cue "Wait".

Leave

There are many ways that you can teach this command, but I have found the following method works well with my Westies.

- Take a treat and place it in your hand, making sure your puppy can sniff it but does not have easy access to take it.

- Hold your hand (with the treat in it) in front of him and command him to "Leave". He may try to 'mug' you, but when he finds this does not work he will go back into the sit position. Immediately praise him.

- Repeat this process a few times until your pup has understood it.

- Now place a treat on the floor and have one treat hidden in your hand. Tell your puppy to "Leave" the treat on the floor, and as soon as he leaves the treat on the floor, reward him with the treat in your hand.

- Put your puppy on the lead and walk him past treats on the floor. Walk right past each treat, commanding him to "Leave". When he responds correctly, reward him with praise and a treat.

The ideal owner

An ideal Westie owner is someone who has time to spend with their dog each day – an owner who can enjoy every minute of a Westie's special brand of companionship and devotion.

Of course, this ideal is rarely possible and Westies find excellent homes with those who manage to be at home at some time during the day.

The main requirement is that a Westie should never be abandoned all day long. He needs human contact, mental stimulation and exercise. A Westie also needs to learn his place in the family pack. He needs to understand where his boundaries lie and respect his fellow pack members. You must establish this relationship with firmness, fairness and consistency so your Westie always knows what is being asked of him and is happy to accept your leadership.

Opportunities for Westies

If you have enjoyed training your Westie, you may want to take his education a step further and try some more advanced exercises, or you may want to get involved with one of the many dog sports that are now on offer.

Agility

This is great fun to watch and join in. Against the clock, at the fastest speed they can muster, dogs jump over obstacles, through tires and tunnels, and negotiate the contact equipment, which includes an A frame, a dog walk and a seesaw.

The Westie competes in classes for small dogs, where the height of the jumps is reduced. If you can get your Westie motivated, he will do surprisingly well at this sport.

Obedience

If your Westie has mastered basic obedience, you may want to get involved in competitive obedience. The exercises include: heelwork at varying paces with dog and handler following a pattern decided by the judge, stays, recalls, retrieves, sendaways, scent discrimination and distance control. The exercises get progressively harder as you progress up the classes.

A Westie will readily learn the exercises that are used in obedience competitions, but, at the top level, a very high degree of precision and accuracy is called for, which some Westies may find too exacting.

Dancing with dogs

This sport is becoming increasingly popular and some Westies have performed with distinction. Dog and handler must perform a choreographed routine to music, which includes a variety of tricks and moves. Routines are judged on style, presentation, content and accuracy.

Good citizen scheme

This scheme is run by national kennel clubs to promote responsible ownership and to train dogs to be well-behaved members of the community. Most training clubs run good citizen classes, which will give you and your dog the opportunity to socialize, as well receive advice on how to get the best from your dog. In the UK there are four stages to the scheme: puppy foundation, bronze, silver, and finally the gold level, which has the most advanced exercises; in the US, there is a single test.

To be a good citizen, your Westie must learn the following exercises:

- Walking on a loose lead among people and other dogs.

- Recall amid distractions.

- A controlled greeting where dogs stay under control while owners meet.

Dogs are sometimes dressed to look the part for dance routines .

- The dog allows all-over grooming and handling by its owner, and also accepts being handled by the examiner.

- Stays, with the owner in sight, and then out of sight.

- Food manners, allowing the owner to eat without begging, and taking a treat on command.

- Sendaway – sending the dog to his bed.

Showing

Showing has its ups and downs, but remember the harder you work at it, the luckier you will become. When you start showing with your Westie, bear in mind it is the judge's personal opinion, so do not take it to heart.

At some shows you will do better than others, but remember to always smile and congratulate the winners, as one day your time will come. Showing must be a fun experience for you and your dog; there is no point showing if you get upset and miserable every time it does not go your way.

On a more positive note, showing can open up a whole new world for you. New friends can be made and you can discover new places to go.

Before you start showing, go to a few shows and watch the other competitors, so you can get a general idea of what happens.

It is best to start showing at open shows so you can gain confidence before attempting a Championship show, which can be pretty nerve-racking. Talk to your fellow exhibitors to obtain advice; you can also ask the breeder of your dog for help.

Showing is highly competitive at the top level, but the dream is to make your Westie into a Show Champion

Earthdog trials

The American Kennel Club run earthdog trials which are specifically designed to test the working ability of the small-legged terriers that were bred to "go to earth" in search of quarry. Man-made tunnels are created, and the dog must work the tunnels in order to find the quarry, which he will indicate by barking, scratching, or digging.

The quarry (usually two rats) are protected by wooden bars across the end of the tunnel so they are not endangered. The Westie is a keen competitor and relishes the opportunity to use his natural talents.

|Health care

We are fortunate that the Westie is
a tough, no-nonsense dog, and with
good routine care, a well-balanced
diet, and sufficient exercise, most will
experience few health problems.

However, it is your responsibility to put a program of
preventative health care in place – and this should
start from the moment your puppy, or older dog,
arrives in his new home.

Vaccinations

Dogs are subject to a number of contagious
diseases. In the old days, these were killers,
and resulted in heartbreak for many owners.
Vaccinations have now been developed, and the
occurrence of the major infectious diseases is now
very rare. However, this will only remain the case
if all pet owners follow a strict policy of vaccinating
their dogs.

Adenovirus: This attacks the liver. Affected dogs have a classic 'blue eye'.

Distemper: A viral disease which causes chest and gastro-intestinal damage. The brain may also be affected, leading to fits and paralysis.

Parvovirus: Causes severe gastro enteritis, and most commonly affects puppies.

Leptospirosis: This bacterial disease is carried by rats and affects many mammals, including humans. It causes liver and kidney damage.

Rabies: A virus that affects the nervous system and is invariably fatal. The first signs are abnormal behavior when the infected dog may bite another animal or a person. Paralysis and death follow. Vaccination is compulsory in most countries. In the UK, dogs travelling overseas must be vaccinated.

Kennel Cough: There are several strains of Kennel Cough, but they all result in a harsh, dry, cough. This disease is rarely fatal; in fact most dogs make a good recovery within a matter of weeks and show few signs of ill health while they are affected. However, kennel cough is highly infectious among dogs that live together so, for this reason, most boarding kennels will insist that your dog is protected by the vaccine, which is given as nose drops.

Lyme Disease: This is a bacterial disease transmitted by ticks (see page 165). The first signs are limping, but the heart, kidneys and nervous system can also be affected. The ticks that transmit the disease occur in specific regions, such as the north-east states of the USA, some of the southern states, California and the upper Mississippi region. Lyme disease is still rare in the UK so vaccinations are not routinely offered.

Vaccination program

In the UK, vaccinations are routinely given for distemper, adenovirus, leptospirosis and parvo virus. In the USA, the American Animal Hospital Association advises vaccination for core diseases, which they list as: distemper, adenovirus, parvovirus and rabies. The requirement for vaccinating for non-core diseases – leptospriosis, Lyme disease and kennel cough – should be assessed depending on a dog's individual risk and his likely exposure to the disease.

In most cases, a puppy will start his vaccinations at around eight weeks of age, with the second part given in a fortnight's time. However, this does vary depending on the individual policy of veterinary practices, and the incidence of disease in your area.

You should also talk to your vet about whether to give annual booster vaccinations. This depends on an individual dog's levels of immunity, and how long a particular vaccine remains effective.

Parasites

No matter how well you look after your Westie, you will have to accept that parasites – internal and external – are ever present, and you need to take preventative action.

Internal parasites: As the name suggests, these parasites live inside your dog. Most will find a home in the digestive tract, but there is also a parasite that lives in the heart. If infestation is unchecked, a dog's health will be severely jeopardized, but routine preventative treatment is simple and effective.

External parasites: These parasites live on your dog's body – in his skin and fur, and sometimes in his ears.

Roundworm

This is found in the small intestine, and signs of infestation will be a poor coat, a pot belly, diarrhoea and lethargy. Pregnant mothers should be treated, but it is almost inevitable that parasites will be passed on to the puppies. For this reason, a breeder will start a worming programme, which you will need to continue. Ask your vet for advice on treatment, which will need to continue throughout your dog's life.

Tapeworm

Infection occurs when fleas and lice are ingested; the adult worm takes up residence in the small intestine, releasing mobile segments (which contain eggs) which can be seen in a dog's feces as small rice-like grains. The only other obvious sign of infestation is irritation of the anus. Again, routine preventative treatment is required throughout your Westie's life.

Heartworm

This parasite is transmitted by mosquitoes, and so it is more likely to be present in areas with a warm, humid climate.

However, it is found in all parts of the USA, although its prevalence does vary, and while heartworm is rarely seen in the UK at present, it pays to be aware of the condition.

Heartworms live in the right side of the heart and larvae can grow up to 14 in (35 cm) in length. A dog with heartworm is at severe risk from heart failure, so preventative treatment, as advised by your vet, is essential. Dogs living in the USA should also have regular tests to check for the presence of infection.

Lungworm

Lungworm, or Angiostrongylus vasorum, is a parasite that lives in the heart and major blood vessels supplying the lungs. It can cause many problems, such as breathing difficulties, excessive bleeding, sickness and diarrhoea, seizures, and can even be fatal. The parasite is carried by slugs and snails, and the dog becomes infected when ingesting these, often accidentally when rummaging through undergrowth. Lungworm is not common, but it is on the increase and a responsible owner should be aware of it. Fortunately, it is easily preventable and even affected dogs usually make a full recovery if treated early enough. Your vet will be able to advise you on the risks in your area and what form of treatment may be required.

Fleas

A dog may carry dog fleas, cat fleas, and even human fleas. The flea stays on the dog only long enough to have a blood meal and to breed, but its presence will result in itching and scratching. If your dog has an allergy to fleas – which is usually a reaction to the flea's saliva – he will scratch himself until he is raw.

Spot-on treatment, administered on a routine basis, is easy to use and highly effective on all fleas.

You can also treat your dog with a spray or with insecticidal shampoo. The whole environment your dog lives in will need to be sprayed, and all other pets living in your home will also need to be treated.

How to detect fleas

You may suspect your dog has fleas, but how can you be sure? There are two methods to try.

Run a fine comb through your dog's coat, and see if you can detect the presence of fleas on the skin, or clinging to the comb. Alternatively, sit your dog on some white paper and rub his back. This will dislodge feces from the fleas, which will be visible as small brown specks. To double check, shake the specks on to some damp cotton wool (cotton). Flea feces consists of the dried blood taken from the host, so if the specks turn a lighter shade of red, you know your dog has fleas.

Ticks

These are blood-sucking parasites which are most frequently found in rural area where sheep or deer are present. The main danger is their ability to pass Lyme disease (see page 159) to both dogs and humans.

The treatment you give your dog for fleas generally works for ticks, but you should discuss the best product to use with your vet.

How to remove a tick

If you spot a tick on your dog, do not try to pluck it off as you risk leaving the hard mouth parts embedded in his skin. The best way to remove a tick is to use a fine pair of tweezers or you can buy a tick remover. Grasp the tick head firmly and then pull the tick straight out from the skin. If you are using a tick remover, check the instructions, as some recommend a circular twist when pulling. When you have removed the tick, clean the area with mild soap and water.

Ear mites

These parasites live in the outer ear canal. The signs of infestation are a brown, waxy discharge, and your dog will continually shake his head and scratch his ear. If you suspect your Westie has ear mites, a visit to the vet will be needed so that medicated ear drops can be prescribed.

Fur mites

These small, white parasites are visible to the naked eye and are often referred to as 'walking dandruff'. They cause a scurfy coat and mild itchiness. However, they are zoonotic – transferable to humans – so prompt treatment with an insecticide prescribed by your vet is essential.

Harvest mites

These are picked up from the undergrowth, and can be seen as a bright orange patch on the webbing between the toes, although this can also be found elsewhere on the body, such as on the ears flaps. Treatment is effective with the appropriate insecticide.

Skin mites

There are two types of parasite that burrow into a dog's skin. Demodex canis is transferred from a mother to her pups while they are feeding. Treatment is with a topical preparation, and sometimes antibiotics are needed.

The other skin mite is sarcoptes scabiei, which causes intense itching and hair loss. It is highly contagious, so all dogs in a household will need to be treated, which involves repeated bathing with a medicated shampoo.

Common ailments

As with all living animals, dogs can be affected by a variety of ailments, most of which can be treated effectively after consulting with your vet, who will prescribe appropriate medication and will advise you on how to care for your Westie's needs.

Here are some of the more common problems that could affect your Westie, with advice on how to deal with them.

Anal glands

These are two small sacs on either side of the anus, which produce a dark-brown secretion that dogs use when they mark their territory.

The anal glands should empty every time a dog defecates but, if they become blocked or impacted, a dog will experience increasing discomfort. He may nibble at his rear end, or 'scoot' his bottom along the ground to relieve the irritation.

Treatment involves a trip to the vet where the vet will empty the glands manually. It is important to do this without delay or infection may occur.

Dental problems

Good dental hygiene will do much to minimize problems with gum infection and tooth decay. If tartar accumulates to the extent that you cannot remove it by brushing, the vet will need to intervene. In a situation such as this, an anesthetic will need to be administered so the tartar can be removed manually.

Diarrhoea

There are many reasons why a dog has diarrhoea, but most commonly it is the result of scavenging, a sudden change of diet, or an adverse reaction to a particular type of food. The Westie has a tough constitution, but digestive upset caused by scavenging is not unusual.

If your dog is suffering from diarrhoea, the first step is to withdraw food for a day. It is important that he does not dehydrate, so make sure that fresh drinking water is available. However, drinking too much can increase the diarrhoea, which may be accompanied with vomiting, so limit how much he drinks at any one time.

After allowing the stomach to rest, feed a bland diet, such as white fish or chicken with boiled rice, for a few days. In most cases, your dog's motions will return to normal and you can resume normal feeding, although this should be done gradually.

However, if this fails to work and the diarrhoea persists for more than a few days, you should consult you vet. Your dog may have an infection, which needs to be treated with antibiotics, or the diarrhoea may indicate some other problem which needs expert diagnosis.

Ear infections

The Westie has small, erect ears, which allow the air to circulate, and so they have relatively few problems with ears infections. However, it is advisable to keep a regular check on your Westie's ears as a problem spotted early on will be much easier to resolve.

A healthy ear is clean with no sign of redness or inflammation, and no evidence of a waxy brown discharge or a foul odor. If you see your dog scratching his ear, shaking his head, or holding one ear at an odd angle, you will need to consult your vet.

The most likely causes are ear mites (see page 166), an infection, or there may a foreign body, such as a grass seed, trapped in the ear.

Depending on the cause, treatment is with medicated ear drops, possibly containing antibiotics. If a foreign body is suspected, the vet will need to carry our further investigations.

Eye problems

The Westie's eyes are deep set, and spaced wide apart; they do not protrude, as in breeds like the Pug, so they are not vulnerable to injury.

However, if your Westie's eyes look red and sore, he may be suffering from conjunctivitis. This may, or may not be accompanied with a watery or a

crusty discharge. Conjunctivitis can be caused by a bacterial or viral infection, it could be the result of an injury, or it could be an adverse reaction to pollen.

You will need to consult your vet for a correct diagnosis, but in the case of an infection, treatment with medicated eye drops is effective.

Conjunctivitis may also be the first sign of more serious inherited eye problems, see page 187.

Foreign bodies

In the home, puppies – and some older dogs – cannot resist chewing anything that looks interesting. The toys you choose for your dog should be suitably robust to withstand damage, but children's toys can be irresistible. Some dogs will chew – and swallow – anything from socks, tights, and other items from the laundry basket, to golf balls and stones from the garden. Obviously, these items are indigestible and could cause an obstruction in your dog's intestine, which is potentially lethal.

The signs to look for are vomiting, and a tucked up posture. The dog will often be restless and will look as though he is in pain. In this situation, you must get your dog to the vet without delay as surgery will be needed to remove the obstruction.

The other type of foreign body that may cause problems is grass seed. A grass seed can enter an orifice such as a nostril, down an ear, the gap between the eye and the eyelid, or penetrate the soft skin between the toes. It can also be swallowed.

The introduction of a foreign body induces a variety of symptoms, depending on the point of entry and where it travels to. The signs to look for include head shaking/ear scratching, the eruption of an abscess, sore, inflamed eyes, or a persistent cough. The vet will be able to make a proper diagnosis, and surgery may be required.

Heatstroke

The Westie is a hardy breed but care should be taken on hot days as heatstroke is a potential danger. When the temperature rises, make sure your dog always has access to shady areas, and wait for a cooler part of the day before going for a walk. Be extra careful if you leave your Westie in the car, as the temperature can rise dramatically – even on a cloudy day. Heatstroke can happen very rapidly, and unless you are able lower your dog's temperature, it can be fatal.

If your Westie appears to be suffering from heatstroke, lie him flat and then cool him as quickly as possible by hosing him, covering him with wet towels, or using frozen food bags from the freezer. As soon as he has made some recovery, take him to the vet where cold intravenous fluids can be administered.

Lameness/limping

There are a wide variety of reasons why a dog can go lame, from a simple muscle strain to a fracture, ligament damage, or more complex problems with the joints which may be an inherited disorder (see pages 182). It takes an expert to make a correct diagnosis, so if you are concerned about your dog, do not delay in seeking help.

As your Westie becomes elderly, he may suffer from arthritis, which you will see as general stiffness, particularly when he gets up after resting. It will help if you ensure his bed is in a warm, draught-free location, and, if your Westie gets wet after exercise, you must dry him thoroughly.

If your elderly Westie seems to be in pain, consult your vet who will be able to help with pain relief medication.

Skin problems

If your dog is scratching or nibbling at his skin, the first thing to check for is fleas (see page 163).There are other external parasites which cause itching and hair loss, but you will need a vet to help you find the culprit.

An allergic reaction is another major cause of skin problems. It can be quite an undertaking to find the cause of the allergy, and you will need to follow your vet's advice, which often requires eliminating specific ingredients from the diet, as well as looking at environmental factors.

Inherited
disorders

The West Highland White Terrier does
have a few breed-related disorders,
and if diagnosed with any of the
diseases listed below, it is important
to remember that they can affect
offspring, so breeding from affected
dogs should be discouraged.

There are now recognized screening tests to enable breeders to check for affected individuals and hence reduce the prevalence of these diseases within the breed, which are mentioned in the following information.

DNA testing is also becoming more widely available, and as research into the different genetic diseases progresses, more DNA tests are being developed.

Patellar luxation

The patellar (knee cap) is situated in the centre of the knee joint; it is held in place by ligaments as it rests in the groove of the femur. Patellar luxation occurs when the knee cap slips out of its normal place. This condition is thought to be inherited due to weak ligaments not holding the patellar in place, but it can be caused by a torn ligament after excessive jumping.

The dog will often start to limp and may go totally lame, holding his hock in a outwards position. Sometimes the patellar can be manually manipulated back into place but it may slip out again in the future. Surgical treatment will resolve the problem completely.

Craniomandibular osteopathy (CMO)

This is an abnormal growth of bone on the lower jaw of the dog. It can be quiet noticeable as the bone that grows out is hard and dense, and has a rough surface. CMO is inherited as an auotosomal trait, which means both parents will be carrying at least one CMO gene.

It only occurs in puppies, normally between the ages of four to ten months, but has been seen as early as four weeks old. It can be very painful for a puppy and he will show discomfort while eating. A high percentage of dogs will recover but the treatment may last a long time, which is why it is best to discuss what course of action to take with your vet.

Cleft palate

Although not common, cleft palate can be seen in all breeds of dogs. It is thought to be inherited, but can occur due to exposure to certain drugs during pregnancy. Cleft palate starts in the womb of the mother and will only affect newborn puppies. The disorder occurs when two bones in the upper ridge of the puppy's mouth do not fuse together leaving a hole in the centre.

If a puppy has cleft palate he will not be able to feed, as when he suckles the milk enters his respiratory passage. Puppies with the disorder will often have milk dripping out of their nostrils. Puppies can only be saved if they are tube-fed and later undergo major surgery. Euthanasia is often advised as it is not fair to put a puppy through major surgery.

Legg-calve-perthes disease

Perthes can occur in the rear legs of your dog. It happens when the blood supply to the tip of the femur is lost. This will result in the death of bone cells in the tip of the femur. New bone may form, but may collapse creating a rough, uneven fit into the hip socket. Perthes only affects young dogs between the ages of three and twelve months.

The symptoms of the disease can take a few weeks to progress. At first your dog may start to walk with a slight limp; after a week or so you may find him to be completely lame, due to the slow progression of the disease. This can be very painful for a puppy so veterinary advice should be sought as soon as possible.

An operation is available to correct the condition, and you will find that your dog will be able to walk perfectly again after a few months of healing.

This disease is primarily seen in small dog breeds, but its cause is not entirely understood. It may be inherited, the result of injury, or even due to a deficiency in the diet. To help eliminate potential problems, affected dogs should not be bred from.

Keratoconjunctivitis sicca (dry eye)

Dry eye is a painful condition that can appear in your dog from the age of four weeks to twelve years, but normally appears before the age of five years.

The disease occurs due to decreased tear production to the eye. Without the presence of tears, the eye will become irritated and the area around the eye will become red and inflamed. The dog may be continually squinting due to intense pain and inflammation. A gooey, sticky discharge will also be present around the eye.

This is a serious condition which, if left untreated, can lead to blindness. You will need to get advice and treatment from your vet, as the affected eyes will need continuous cleaning and the administration of artificial tears. Antibiotics may be needed and in severe cases surgery may be required.

Summing up

It may give the pet owner cause for concern to find about health problems that may affect their dog. But it is important to bear in mind that acquiring some basic knowledge is an asset, as it will allow you to spot signs of trouble at an early stage. Early diagnosis is very often the means to the most effective treatment.

Fortunately, the Westie is a generally healthy and disease-free dog with his only visits to the vet being for an annual check-up. In most cases, owners can look forward to enjoying many happy years with this loyal and spirited companion.

Useful addresses

Breed & Kennel Clubs

Please contact your Kennel Club to obtain contact information about breed clubs in your area.

UK

The Kennel Club (UK)
1 Clarges Street London, W1J 8AB
Telephone: 0870 606 6750
Fax: 0207 518 1058
Web: www.thekennelclub.org.uk

USA

American Kennel Club (AKC)
5580 Centerview Drive, Raleigh, NC 27606.
Telephone: 919 233 9767
Fax: 919 233 3627
Email: info@akc.org
Web: www.akc.org

United Kennel Club (UKC)
100 E Kilgore Rd, Kalamazoo,
MI 49002-5584, USA.
Tel: 269 343 9020
Fax: 269 343 7037
Web:www.ukcdogs.com/

Australia

Australian National Kennel Council (ANKC)
The Australian National Kennel Council is the administrative body for pure breed canine affairs in Australia. It does not, however, deal directly with dog exhibitors, breeders or judges. For information pertaining to breeders, clubs or shows, please contact the relevant State or Territory Body.

International

Fédération Cynologique Internationalé (FCI)
Place Albert 1er, 13, B-6530 Thuin, Belgium.
Tel: +32 71 59.12.38
Fax: +32 71 59.22.29
Web: www.fci.be/

Training and behavior

UK

Association of Pet Dog Trainers
Telephone: 01285 810811
Web: http://www.apdt.co.uk

Association of Pet Behaviour Counsellors
Telephone: 01386 751151
Web: http://www.apbc.org.uk/

USA

Association of Pet Dog Trainers
Tel: 1 800 738 3647
Web: www.apdt.com/

American College of Veterinary Behaviorists
Web: http://dacvb.org/

American Veterinary Society of Animal Behavior
Web: www.avsabonline.org/

Australia

APDT Australia Inc
Web: www.apdt.com.au

Canine Behavior
For details of regional behaviorists, contact the relevant State or Territory Controlling Body.

Activities
UK
Agility Club
http://www.agilityclub.co.uk/

British Flyball Association
Telephone: 01628 829623
Web: http://www.flyball.org.uk/

USA
North American Dog Agility Council
Web: www.nadac.com/

North American Flyball Association, Inc.
Tel/Fax: 800 318 6312
Web: www.flyball.org/

Australia
Agility Dog Association of Australia
Tel: 0423 138 914
Web: www.adaa.com.au/

NADAC Australia
Web: www.nadacaustralia.com/

Australian Flyball Association
Tel: 0407 337 939
Web: www.flyball.org.au/

International
World Canine Freestyle Organisation
Tel: (718) 332-8336
Web: www.worldcaninefreestyle.org

Health
UK
British Small Animal Veterinary Association
Tel: 01452 726700
Web: http://www.bsava.com/

Royal College of Veterinary Surgeons
Tel: 0207 222 2001
Web: www.rcvs.org.uk

www.dogbooksonline.co.uk/healthcare/

Alternative Veterinary Medicine Centre
Tel: 01367 710324
Web: www.alternativevet.org/

USA
American Veterinary Medical Association
Tel: 800 248 2862
Web: www.avma.org

American College of Veterinary Surgeons
Tel: 301 916 0200
Toll Free: 877 217 2287
Web: www.acvs.org/

Canine Eye Registration Foundation
The Veterinary Medical Databases
1717 Philo Rd, PO Box 3007,
Urbana, IL 61803-3007
Tel: 217-693-4800
Fax: 217-693-4801
Web: http://www.vmdb.org/cerf.html

Orthopaedic Foundation of Animals
2300 E Nifong Boulevard
Columbia, Missouri, 65201-3806
Tel: 573 442-0418
Fax: 573 875-5073
Web: http://www.offa.org/

American Holistic Veterinary Medical
Association
Tel: 410 569 0795
Web: www.ahvma.org/

Australia
Australian Small Animal Veterinary
Association
Tel: 02 9431 5090
Web: www.asava.com.au

Australian Veterinary Association
Tel: 02 9431 5000
Web: www.ava.com.au

Australian College Veterinary Scientists
Tel: 07 3423 2016
Web: http://acvsc.org.au

Australian Holistic Vets
Web: www.ahv.com.au/